Super Easy
SWEETS

69 REALLY SIMPLE DESSERT RECIPES

NATACHA ARNOULT

PHOTOGRAPHS BY VALÉRY GUEDES

CLARKSON POTTER/PUB
NEW YORK

D1404128

Contents

TARTS

CREAMY TREATS

FROZEN DESSERTS

POUND CAKE

 10 minutes prep time

 40 minutes baking time

 Serves 4

butter, room temperature
1 cup, plus 2 tablespoons

flour
1¾ cups, plus 2 tablespoons

sugar
1 cup

eggs
x 4

yeast
1¼-ounce package

○ Preheat the oven to 350°F. Butter and flour an 8-inch springform cake pan, using 2 tablespoons of each ingredient.

○ In a large bowl, cream the remaining 1 cup butter and the sugar. Then beat the eggs in one at a time, and add the yeast and the remaining 1¾ cups flour.

○ Pour the batter into the pan and bake for 15 minutes. Reduce the heat to 300°F and bake for 25 minutes more. Check for doneness using a toothpick.

cakes

DUTCH BABY

 15 minutes prep time

 20 minutes baking time

 Serves 4

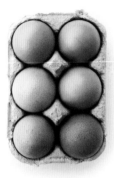

eggs
x 2

crème fraîche
½ cup

whole milk
½ cup

flour
1 cup

sugar
2½ tablespoons

unsalted butter
2 tablespoons

O Preheat the oven to 425°F.

O In a large bowl, combine the eggs, crème fraîche, milk, flour, and sugar.

O Melt the butter in an 8- or 9-inch oven-safe skillet. Pour the batter into the skillet and bake for 20 minutes, until the whole pancake puffs up then collapses in the center.

O Serve with honey, maple syrup, or seasonal fruit, if desired.

HAZELNUT CAKE

15 minutes prep time

30 minutes baking time

Serves 4

butter
⅔ cup, plus 2 tablespoons

flour
⅔ cup

sugar
1 cup

hazelnuts, ground
1½ cups

egg whites
x 5

○ Preheat the oven to 350°F and grease an 11 x 7-inch cake pan with 2 tablespoons butter.

○ Melt the remaining ⅔ cup butter in a small saucepan over very low heat.

○ In a medium bowl, combine the flour, sugar, and ground hazelnuts. In a separate medium bowl, lightly beat the egg whites, then fold into the flour mixture. Add the warm butter and combine.

○ Pour the batter into the cake pan and bake for about 30 minutes. Check for doneness using a toothpick. Let cool, then dust with powdered sugar, if desired.

YOGURT CAKE

 10 minutes prep time

 40 minutes baking time

 Serves 4

butter
⅔ cup, plus 2 tablespoons

flour
1½ cups, plus 2 tablespoons

plain yogurt
½ cup

Demerara sugar
1 cup

eggs
x 3

yeast
1¼-ounce package

○ Preheat the oven to 350°F. Butter and flour an 8 x 4-inch loaf pan, using 2 tablespoons of each ingredient.

○ Melt the remaining ⅔ cup butter in a small saucepan over very low heat.

○ In a large bowl, combine the yogurt, the remaining 1½ cups flour, the sugar, eggs, butter, and yeast.

○ Pour the batter into the pan and bake for 40 minutes. Check for doneness using a toothpick.

CHOCOLATE FONDANT CAKE

 20 minutes prep time

 20 minutes baking time

 Serves 4

salted butter, room
temperature
⅔ cup, plus 2 tablespoons

flour
8 tablespoons

eggs
x 4

chocolate
8 ounces

sugar
¾ cup

○ Preheat the oven to 400°F. Butter and flour an 8-inch springform cake pan, using 2 tablespoons of each ingredient.

○ Separate the egg yolks and whites. Melt the chocolate in a double boiler, stirring until smooth. Remove from the heat and let cool.

○ In a medium bowl, cream the remaining ⅔ cup butter and sugar. Add the melted chocolate, then the egg yolks. Slowly fold in the remaining 6 tablespoons flour.

○ In a separate medium bowl, beat the egg whites until lightly stiff, then gently fold into the batter. Pour the batter into the cake pan and bake for 20 minutes, or until the center is just set.

NO-BAKE CHOCOLATE CHESTNUT CAKE

15 minutes prep time

No bake

Serves 4

dark chocolate
4½ ounces

chestnut cream
17.6 ounces (1 large can)

butter, room temperature
⅓ cup

○ Line an 8 x 8-inch cake pan with parchment paper.

○ Break the chocolate bar into pieces and melt it in a double boiler, stirring until smooth. Remove from the heat and let cool.

○ Fold in the chestnut cream and butter.

○ Pour the mixture into the cake pan and let it set in the refrigerator for 12 hours.

chocolate
BROWNIES

dark chocolate
14 ounces

salted butter
1¼ cups

Demerara sugar
1½ cups

eggs
x 6

flour
1¼ cups

 10 minutes prep time

 35–40 minutes baking time

 Serves 6

○ Preheat the oven to 350°F and line an 11 x 17-inch baking dish with parchment paper.

○ Melt 11 ounces of the chocolate and the butter in a double boiler, stirring until smooth. Remove from the heat and let cool.

○ Add the sugar, eggs, flour, and a pinch of salt. Stir to combine.

○ Coarsely chop the remaining chocolate and fold it into the batter.

○ Pour the batter into the baking dish and bake for 35–40 minutes. Let cool, then slice into squares and serve.

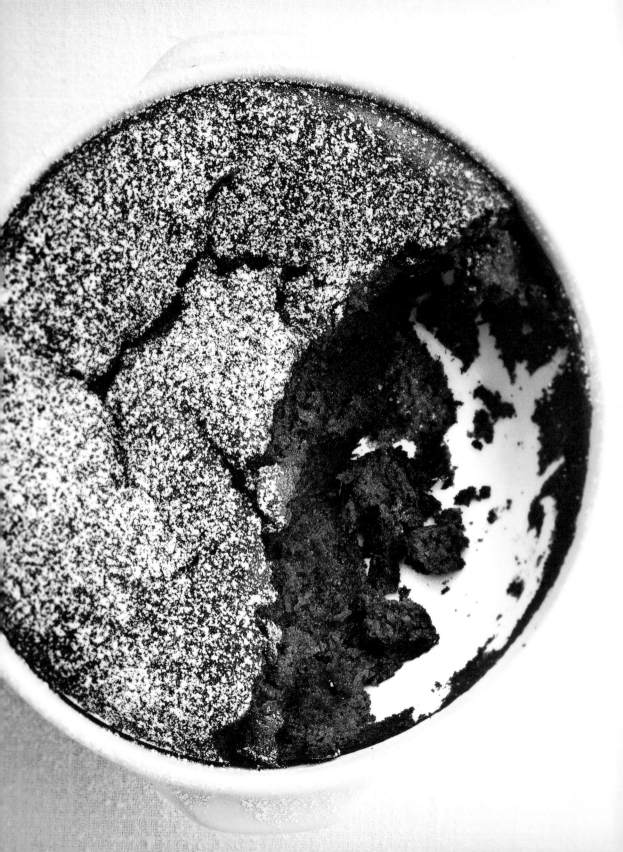

CHOCOLATE CHESTNUT FONDANT CAKE

 20 minutes prep time

 45 minutes baking time

 Serves 6

butter
½ cup, plus 2 tablespoons

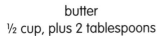

flour
2 tablespoons

eggs
x 4

dark chocolate
4 ounces

chestnut cream
17.6 ounces (1 large can)

○ Preheat the oven to 350°F. Butter and flour a 7-inch round cake pan, using 2 tablespoons of each ingredient.

○ Separate the egg yolks and whites.

○ Melt the remaining ½ cup butter and the chocolate in a double boiler, stirring until smooth. Remove from the heat and let cool, then add in the chestnut cream and the egg yolks.

○ In a medium bowl, beat the egg whites along with a pinch of salt until lightly stiff, then carefully fold into the chocolate-chestnut mixture.

○ Pour the batter into the pan and bake for 45 minutes. Let cool and dust with powdered sugar, if desired.

MOLTEN CHOCOLATE CAKES

 15 minutes prep time

 8–10 minutes baking time

 Serves 4

butter
½ cup, plus 2 tablespoons

sugar
⅓ cup, plus 2 tablespoons

dark chocolate
4½ ounces

eggs
x 2, plus 2 yolks

flour
2½ tablespoons

O Preheat the oven to 400°F. Butter and sugar 4 (3-inch) ramekins using 2 tablespoons of each ingredient, then place them in the refrigerator.

O Melt the chocolate and the remaining ½ cup butter in a double boiler, stirring until smooth. Remove from the heat and let cool.

O In a medium bowl, beat the whole eggs, egg yolks, and the remaining ⅓ cup sugar until it reaches a pale, creamy consistency. Add the chocolate mixture, then the flour. Mix quickly, being careful not to overstir.

O Pour into the ramekins, then bake for 8–10 minutes. The center should not solidify. Let cool and dust with powdered sugar, if desired.

CHOCOLATE TARTS

 20 minutes prep time

 15–20 minutes baking time

 Makes 4 tarts

pie dough
2 sheets, packaged

dark chocolate
9 ounces

heavy cream
1¼ cups

honey
1½ tablespoons

○ Cut the sheets of dough in half and press them into 4 (4-inch) tart pans, then cut off the excess to fit the pan. Refrigerate for 20 minutes.

○ Preheat the oven to 325°F.

○ Bake the crusts for 15–20 minutes.

○ Chop the chocolate and place it in a small bowl. In a small saucepan, bring the cream and honey to a boil, then pour over the chocolate. Let stand for 1 minute, then blend with a spatula. Pour the mixture into the baked tart crusts and let set for 2 hours in a cool place (not in the refrigerator).

○ Sprinkle with the coarse salt to serve.

coarse sea salt
1 pinch

EASY CHOCOLATE MOUSSE

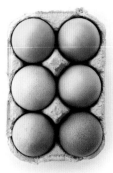

🔪 **15 minutes prep time**

🍲 **No bake**

☺ **Serves 4**

eggs
x 4

dark chocolate
6½ ounces

sugar
⅓ cup

○ Separate the egg yolks and whites. Melt the chocolate in a double boiler, stirring until smooth. Remove from the heat and let cool. Gently fold in the egg yolks with a spatula.

○ In a medium bowl, beat the egg whites along with a pinch of salt until stiff. Gradually add in the sugar while beating. Gently fold the egg white mixture into the chocolate, making sure to not collapse the egg whites.

○ Scoop the mousse into 4 ramekins and refrigerate for 2 hours.

NUTELLA MOUSSE

 10 minutes prep time

No bake

Serves 4

heavy cream
1 cup

Nutella
1 small jar (13 ounces)

hazelnuts
¼ cup

○ In a medium bowl, firmly whip the cream while very cold.

○ Add the Nutella to a separate medium bowl, and fold in 2 tablespoons of the whipped cream to soften it. Carefully fold in the rest of the whipped cream. Scoop the mousse into 4 ramekins and refrigerate for 3 hours.

○ In a small nonstick skillet, toast the hazelnuts. Let cool, then scrape off the skins. Roughly chop the hazelnuts, then sprinkle them over the mousse to serve.

CHOCOLATE RICOTTA ICEBOX CAKE

 20 minutes prep time

No bake

:) **Serves 4**

dark chocolate
13 ounces

ricotta
2 cups

chocolate sugar wafers
1 package

O Line an 8 x 4-inch cake pan with parchment paper.

O Melt 11½ ounces of the chocolate in a double boiler, stirring until smooth. Remove from the heat and let cool to room temperature, then mix in the ricotta.

O Cover the bottom of the lined pan with a layer of the ricotta mixture, then add a layer of chocolate sugar wafers. Continue layering until you run out of ingredients, ending with the ricotta mixture on top.

O Refrigerate for 12 hours. Grate the remaining 1½ ounces chocolate over the cake, then slice to serve.

CHOCO CORNFLAKE TREATS

  15 minutes prep time

 No bake

 **Serves 4**

dark chocolate
7 ounces

salted butter
⅓ cup

○ Line a baking sheet with parchment paper.

○ Melt the chocolate and butter in a double boiler, stirring until smooth. Remove from the heat and let cool.

○ Place the cornflakes in a large bowl, then pour the chocolate over and stir to combine. Form into 4 mounds, then place on the baking sheet.

○ Let set for 1 hour in the refrigerator.

cornflakes
2½ cups

CHOCOLATE TRUFFLES

25 minutes prep time

No bake

Makes 30 truffles

milk or dark chocolate
7 ounces

heavy cream
¾ cup

O Break apart the chocolate and place the chunks in a medium bowl. In a small saucepan, bring the cream to a simmer over low heat. Pour it over the chocolate.

O Wait 1 minute, then gently fold together to ensure a smooth and uniform consistency. Refrigerate for at least 3 hours.

O Mold into 1-inch balls. Place the cocoa powder in a medium bowl and roll the balls to cover.

cocoa powder
2 tablespoons

CHOCOLATE CANDIES

dark chocolate
9 ounces

dried fruits, chopped
½ cup

whole nuts of your choice
½ cup

 30 minutes prep time

 No bake

 Makes 20–30 candies

O Line a baking sheet with parchment paper.

O Break the chocolate up into chunks and melt in a double boiler, stirring until smooth. Remove from the heat and let cool for 3–5 minutes. Spoon out the chocolate onto the baking sheet, making 20–30 discs.

O Place dried fruit and nuts of your choosing on each chocolate disc. Sprinkle lightly with coarse salt, if desired. Let rest in a cool, dry place until the chocolate is set. Remove using a spatula and serve. The candies can be stored in an airtight container in a cool place (but do not refrigerate) for up to 3 days.

AMARETTO COOKIES

 10 minutes prep time

 12–18 minutes baking time

 Makes 20 cookies

blanched almonds
1⅔ cups

sugar
1¼ cups

almond extract
1½ teaspoons

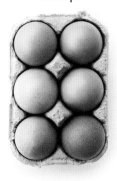

egg whites
x 3

○ Preheat the oven to 375°F and line a baking sheet with parchment paper.

○ In a medium bowl, mix together the almonds and sugar, then stir in the almond extract.

○ In a separate medium bowl, beat the egg whites until lightly stiff, then fold in the almond mixture.

○ Form into 20 small mounds on the baking sheet, spacing them out evenly. For soft cookies, bake for 12–13 minutes, or until golden brown. For crunchier cookies, bake 3–5 minutes more.

SHORTBREAD TART

 15 minutes prep time

 20–30 minutes baking time

 Serves 4

flour
1²/₃ cups

sugar
¼ cup

butter
½ cup

O Preheat the oven to 325°F.

O In a medium bowl, combine the flour and sugar. Cut the butter into small chunks, then mix into the flour and sugar with your fingers to create a crumbly mixture.

O Press the dough into an 8-inch tart pan. Score 10 slices into the dough with a knife (this will make it easier to cut the shortbread once it's baked).

O Bake for 20–30 minutes, until light golden brown. Let cool, then remove from the pan and cut.

SHORTBREAD THINS

 10 minutes prep time

 10 minutes baking time

 Makes 20 cookies

shortbread dough, store-
bought or homemade
(see page 39)
2 sheets

powdered sugar
to garnish

○ Line a baking sheet with parchment paper.

○ Use a cookie cutter or a glass to cut 20 round discs out of the prepared dough and place them on the baking sheet. Refrigerate for 30 minutes.

○ Preheat the oven to 350°F. Bake the cookies for about 10 minutes, until golden brown.

○ Sprinkle with the powdered sugar to serve.

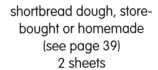

CHOCOLATE CHIP BISCUITS

 **10 minutes prep time**

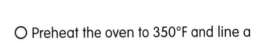 **10–15 minutes baking time**

Makes 30 biscuits

butter, room temperature
⅔ cup

Demerara sugar
1 cup

vanilla extract
½ teaspoon

eggs
x 2

flour
2½ cups

yeast
1 teaspoon

chocolate chips
¾ cup

○ Preheat the oven to 350°F and line a baking sheet with parchment paper.

○ In a medium bowl, combine the butter and sugar, then add the vanilla extract. Beat in the eggs one at a time. Stir in the flour and yeast using a wooden spoon, being careful not to overmix. Gently fold in the chocolate chips.

○ Spoon the dough out onto the baking sheet, spacing them out evenly and lightly flattening the mounds. Bake for 10–15 minutes, or until light brown.

COCONUT MOUNDS

 5 minutes prep time

 5–8 minutes baking time

 Makes 15–20 mounds

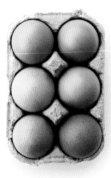

egg whites
x 2

shredded coconut
2 cups

vanilla extract
½ teaspoon

sugar
½ cup

O Preheat the oven to 300°F and line a baking sheet with parchment paper.

O Place the egg whites, coconut, vanilla, and sugar in a medium bowl and mix using your hands.

O Form into 15–20 small mounds using your fingers, then place them on the baking sheet. Bake for 5–8 minutes, or until light golden brown.

PALMIERS

 15 minutes prep time

 10–15 minutes baking time

 Makes 20 palmiers

puff pastry
4 sheets, packaged

Demerara sugar
2 tablespoons

cinnamon
1 tablespoon

egg yolk
x 1

○ Pile the puff pastry sheets on top of one another and press with a rolling pin. Trim the sides of the pastry to make the pastry square. Sprinkle with the sugar and cinnamon. Roll the 2 short sides in toward the center, until touching. Place in the freezer for 30 minutes.

○ Preheat the oven to 400°F and line a baking sheet with parchment paper.

○ In a small bowl, dilute the egg yolk with 1 tablespoon water. Cut the roll into 20 thin slices and place on the baking sheet. Lightly brush each with the egg wash. Return to the freezer for 10 minutes, then bake for 10–15 minutes.

PAIN PERDU

 10 minutes prep time

 8–12 minutes baking time

Serves 4

eggs
x 3

sugar
¼ cup

○ In a medium bowl, beat the eggs, sugar, and vanilla, then stir in the milk.

vanilla extract
1 teaspoon

whole milk
1 pint

○ Soak the slices of bread in the mix one by one, evenly soaking both sides.

○ In a medium skillet, melt the butter over medium heat. Cook 2 slices at a time for 2–3 minutes on each side, until brown and crisp on the edges.

○ Drizzle with honey or maple syrup, if desired.

bread
8 slices

butter
3 tablespoons

BAKED APPLES

15 minutes prep time

1 hour baking time

Serves 4

apples
x 4

apple cider
½ cup

sugar
4 tablespoons

○ Preheat the oven to 300°F.

○ Core the apples and arrange them in a 9-inch baking dish, douse them with the cider, and sprinkle with the sugar.

○ Bake for 1 hour, occasionally spooning the juices over the apples as they cook. Reduce the heat if they start to appear dry.

ORANGE MANGO SALAD

 15 minutes prep time

 No bake

 Serves 4

mango
x 1

oranges
x 2

ginger
1 (1-inch) piece

lime
x 1

honey
3 tablespoons

O Peel and thinly slice the mango and oranges, then place them in a small bowl. Peel and grate the ginger and set aside.

O Finely zest and juice the lime and pour it over the fruit. Drizzle with honey and sprinkle with the grated ginger and lime zest. Gently toss together.

O Let marinate for at least 1 hour in the refrigerator.

COCONUT MELON SALAD

 12 minutes prep time

 No bake

 Serves 4

coconut milk
1 cup

Demerara sugar
1 tablespoon

cantaloupe
x 1

mint
6 leaves, chopped

○ In a small saucepan, heat the coconut milk and sugar over low heat. Remove from the heat as soon as the sugar dissolves, and let cool.

○ Cut the cantaloupe in half, remove the seeds and skin, and cut into slices. Divide the melon slices among 4 shallow bowls.

○ Pour the coconut milk over each, then sprinkle the mint on top. Let them marinate for at least 1 hour in the refrigerator.

POACHED PEARS

vanilla beans
x 2

honey
4 tablespoons

lemon
1 tablespoon

sweet white wine
1 cup

pears
x 8 small

🔪 **20 minutes prep time**

🍲 **45 minutes baking time**

☺ **Serves 4**

○ Preheat the oven to 350°F and lightly grease a 13 x 15-inch baking dish with butter.

○ Cut the vanilla beans lengthwise and scrape out the seeds with a knife. In a small bowl, combine the vanilla seeds, honey, lemon juice, and wine.

○ Peel and halve the pears, then arrange them in the baking dish. Evenly douse with the honey-wine mixture. Cover with parchment paper and bake for 30 minutes, occasionally spooning the juices over the fruit as it cooks.

○ Remove the parchment paper and bake for 15 minutes more.

APPLE DUMPLINGS

 20 minutes prep time

 20–22 minutes baking time

 Makes 4 dumplings

pie dough
2 sheets, packaged

apples
x 4

sugar
2 tablespoons

egg yolks
x 2

O Preheat the oven to 400°F and line an 18 x 13-inch baking dish with parchment paper.

O Thinly roll out the pie dough and cut out 4 rectangles.

O Peel the apples and evenly sprinkle with the sugar. Place an apple on each rectangle of pie dough and fully wrap the dough around the apple, pinching the edges to seal. Arrange in the baking dish.

O In a small bowl, dilute the yolks with 4 tablespoons water. Brush the dough with the egg wash.

O Bake for 5–7 minutes, then reduce the temperature to 350°F and bake for 15 minutes more.

O Let cool for 30 minutes before serving.

TROPICAL POACHED MANGO

 15 minutes prep time

 10 minutes cooking time

 Serves 4

passion fruit
x 12

sweet white wine
¾ cup

sugar
1 cup

mangoes
x 2

○ Slice the passion fruit in half and scoop out the pulp. Strain it through a sieve and place the strained contents in a medium saucepan, then add the wine and the sugar. Bring to a boil over medium-high heat, then reduce the heat to medium and let simmer for 10 minutes.

○ While it's simmering, peel and thinly slice the mangoes. Arrange the mango slices in a medium bowl and pour the warm syrup over them. Let cool to room temperature, then refrigerate for at least 3 hours.

SPIKED FRUIT SALAD

 20 minutes prep time

No bake

Serves 4

pineapple
2 cups

mango
x 1

○ Peel and core the pineapple and mango (if necessary) and cut into chunks, then place in a large bowl with the raspberries. Add the sugar and rum and gently toss to coat.

○ Let marinate for up to 1 hour in a cool place (not in the refrigerator) before serving.

raspberries
2 cups

Demerara sugar
2 tablespoons

rum
3 tablespoons

ROASTED SPICED FRUIT

 15 minutes prep time

 20 minutes baking time

 Serves 4

orange
x 1

lime
x 1

pineapple
x 1

mango
x 1

butter
2 tablespoons

Demerara sugar
2 tablespoons

cinnamon stick
x 1

vanilla beans
x 2

○ Preheat the oven to 400°F.

○ Zest and juice the orange and lime. Peel and core the pineapple and mango (if necessary) and cut into large chunks.

○ Cut the butter into small chunks. Place the fruit and zest in a 13 x 9-inch baking dish and sprinkle evenly with the Demerara sugar and butter. Add a splash of the orange and lime juice, the cinnamon stick, and the whole vanilla beans, then bake for 20 minutes.

fruit

CARAMELIZED BANANAS

 5 minutes prep time

 3–5 minutes cooking time

 Serves 4

bananas
x 4

Demerara sugar or honey
8 tablespoons

butter
3 tablespoons

O Slice the unpeeled bananas in half lengthwise. Sprinkle the cut side of each banana half with 1 tablespoon sugar or drizzle with 1 tablespoon honey.

O Melt the butter in a large skillet over medium-high heat. Caramelize the cut sides of the bananas for 3–5 minutes, or until golden brown.

O Serve with ice cream, if desired.

COCONUT CARAMELIZED PINEAPPLE

 10 minutes prep time

 7–11 minutes cooking time

 Serves 4

pineapple
x 1

sugar (white or Demerara)
½ cup

salted butter
3 tablespoons

shredded coconut
⅓ cup

○ Peel, core, and slice the pineapple.

○ In a large skillet, caramelize the sugar over medium-high heat for 3–5 minutes. Once lightly browned, remove the skillet from the heat and add the butter. Stir to combine, then return to the heat and add the pineapple. Lightly brown for 2–3 minutes on each side.

○ Transfer to a large serving dish and sprinkle with the shredded coconut to serve.

CLAFOUTIS

butter
5 tablespoons

eggs
x 4

 10 minutes prep time

 25–30 minutes baking time

 Serves 4

sugar
⅔ cup

vanilla extract
1 teaspoon

○ Preheat the oven to 400°F and grease a 9-inch round cake pan with 2 tablespoons of the butter.

○ Melt the remaining 3 tablespoons butter in a small saucepan over low heat. In a large bowl, combine the eggs, sugar, and vanilla. Then add in the flour, cream, milk, and melted butter.

○ Pour the batter into the baking dish, top with the cherries, and bake for 25–30 minutes. Let cool and sprinkle with powdered sugar, if desired.

flour
¾ cup

heavy cream
¾ cup

whole milk
¾ cup

cherries
1 pound, frozen

APPLE-MANGO CRUMBLE

 15 minutes prep time

 35 minutes baking time

 Serves 4

mango
x 1

apples
x 4

butter
½ cup

flour
1 cup

cinnamon
1 teaspoon

Demerara sugar
⅔ cup

○ Preheat the oven to 350°F.

○ Peel and roughly chop the mango and apples and place in 4 small ramekins.

○ Cut the butter into chunks, then in a medium bowl, combine the flour, cinnamon, sugar, and butter using your fingers.

○ Cover the fruit with the crumble and bake for about 35 minutes, or until the crumble topping is golden brown at the edges.

fruit

RHUBARB CRISP

rhubarb
2 pounds

sugar
¾ cup

 15 minutes prep time

 30–35 minutes baking time

 Serves 4

butter
6 tablespoons

flour
¾ cup

○ Preheat the oven to 350°F.

○ Peel and chop the rhubarb. In a medium saucepan, stew the rhubarb and ¼ cup of the sugar over medium heat for 10 minutes. Transfer it to a 6-inch baking dish.

○ Cut the butter into chunks. In a medium bowl, combine the flour, remaining ½ cup sugar, ground almonds, and butter using your fingers.

○ Cover the rhubarb with the crumble and bake for 30–35 minutes. Serve warm with ice cream or crème fraîche, if desired.

almonds, ground
⅔ cup

DECONSTRUCTED BANOFFEE PIE

15 minutes prep time

No bake

Serves 4

small meringues
x 8, packaged

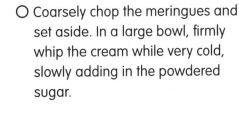
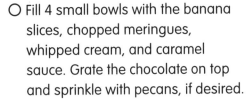

heavy cream
¾ cup

powdered sugar
1 tablespoon

bananas, sliced
x 2

caramel sauce
4 tablespoons

chocolate
4 tablespoons

○ Coarsely chop the meringues and set aside. In a large bowl, firmly whip the cream while very cold, slowly adding in the powdered sugar.

○ Fill 4 small bowls with the banana slices, chopped meringues, whipped cream, and caramel sauce. Grate the chocolate on top and sprinkle with pecans, if desired.

COCONUT BERRY CREAM

 15 minutes prep time

No bake

 Serves 4

lime
x ½

mixed berries
6 cups

sugar
1 tablespoon

heavy cream
⅔ cup

powdered sugar
1 tablespoon

coconut cream
½ cup

shredded coconut
1 tablespoon

○ Finely zest and juice the lime. If using strawberries, destem and cut in half.

○ In a medium bowl, mix the berries with the sugar, lime juice and zest. Let marinate for 30 minutes.

○ In a medium bowl, firmly whip the cream while very cold, slowly adding in the powdered sugar and coconut cream.

○ Serve the berries with the coconut whipped cream. Top with the shredded coconut.

FRUIT TRIFLE

✎ **20 minutes prep time**

🍲 **No bake**

☺ **Serves 4**

shortbread cookies
x 8

peaches
x 4, canned

○ Coarsely chop the cookies and cut the peaches into chunks. In a medium bowl, firmly whip the cream and mascarpone while very cold, slowly adding in the powdered sugar.

heavy cream
⅔ cup

mascarpone
1 tablespoon

○ Place 2 cookies in the bottom of 4 glasses or small bowls. Then add the peaches and berries and top with the mascarpone cream.

○ Refrigerate for at least 2 hours.

powdered sugar
2 tablespoons

mixed berries
2 cups

ETON MESS

🔪 **15 minutes prep time**

🍲 **No bake**

☺ **Serves 4**

mixed berries
4 cups

small meringues
x 8, packaged

heavy cream
¾ cup

powdered sugar
1 tablespoon

○ If using strawberries, destem and cut in half, then combine with the other berries in a large bowl. Coarsely chop the meringues and set aside.

○ In a medium bowl, firmly whip the cream while very cold, slowly adding in the powdered sugar.

○ Layer the meringues, whipped cream, and berries in 4 small bowls or ramekins, finishing with the cream on top.

BERRY CUSTARD

 15 minutes prep time

 2 minutes baking time

 Serves 4

mixed berries
3 cups

lemon
x ½

egg yolks
x 3

sugar
⅓ cup

vanilla bean
x 1

heavy cream
⅔ cup

O Set the oven to broil.

O If using strawberries, destem and cut in half, then place all the berries in 4 small heat-resistant bowls or ramekins.

O Zest and juice the lemon. Split the vanilla bean lengthwise and scrape out the seeds. In a medium bowl, beat the egg yolks and sugar for 8–10 minutes, until it reaches a pale, creamy consistency. Then stir in the seeds, and the lemon zest and juice. Pour in the cream, whipping as you do so.

O Divide the mixture among the 4 bowls. Broil for 2 minutes or use a culinary torch to caramelize the top.

PINEAPPLE FLAN

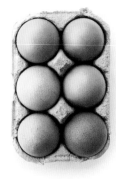

20 minutes prep time

30–45 minutes baking time

Serves 4

cornstarch
1 tablespoon

eggs
x 5

pineapple
1 can (20 ounces)

sugar
¼ cup

○ Preheat the oven to 300°F.

○ In a small bowl, dissolve the cornstarch in 2 tablespoons water. In a medium bowl, lightly beat the eggs. Strain the pineapple and pulse in a blender. In a small saucepan, bring the pineapple and sugar to a boil over medium-high heat. Immediately remove from the heat and let cool, then stir in the liquid cornstarch and the eggs.

○ Pour the caramel sauce into a 9-inch round cake pan, then pour the pineapple mixture over the top. Place the pan in a larger baking dish filled halfway with hot water, being careful not to submerge the pan. Bake for 45 minutes. Let cool to room temperature, then refrigerate for at least 6 hours. Serve caramel-side up.

caramel sauce
6 tablespoons

COUNTRY FRUIT GALETTE

 20 minutes prep time

 30–40 minutes baking time

 Serves 4

pie dough
1 sheet, packaged

seasonal fruit
1 pound

Demerara sugar
2 tablespoons

○ Preheat the oven to 350°F and line a baking sheet with parchment paper.

○ Unroll the pie dough and place it on the baking sheet.

○ Peel, core, and slice the fruit. Evenly distribute it on the pie dough, leaving 2–3 inches of space around the edges. Sprinkle evenly with the sugar.

○ Fold the edges of the dough over the fruit and bake for 30–40 minutes.

EASY MINI LEMON TARTS

 10 minutes prep time

 1 minute baking time

 Makes 8 mini tarts

lemon curd (see page 101)
2 tablespoons

shortbread cookies
x 8

egg whites
x 2

sugar
½ cup

○ Set the oven to broil and line a baking sheet with parchment paper.

○ Spread the lemon curd on the shortbread cookies and evenly space on the baking sheet.

○ In a medium bowl, beat the egg whites until lightly stiff, add the sugar, and continue beating for several minutes more to create a meringue.

○ Add a dollop of meringue to each mini tart. Broil for 1 minute or until the meringue topping is very lightly browned.

TARTE TATIN

✎ **20 minutes prep time**

🍲 **28 minutes baking time**

☺ **Serves 4**

caramel sauce
6 tablespoons

apples
x 8

butter
3 tablespoons

pie dough
1 sheet, packaged

○ Preheat the oven to 375°F.

○ Pour the caramel sauce into a 9-inch round cake pan or pie plate. Peel and core the apples, then cut them into quarters.

○ In a medium skillet, melt the butter over medium heat, then brown the apples for 8 minutes.

○ Layer the browned apples on top of the caramel. Cover with the pie dough and tuck the edges into the pan.

○ Bake for about 20 minutes, or until the crust turns golden brown and the caramel seeps up the sides.

○ Let cool for 15–20 minutes before removing from the pan. Serve with ice cream or crème fraîche, if desired.

FAST FRUIT TARTS

✎ **20 minutes prep time**

⊔ **15 minutes baking time**

☺ **Serves 4**

puff pastry
2 sheets, packaged

mixed berries
2 cups

○ Preheat the oven to 350°F and line a baking sheet with parchment paper.

○ Cut out 8 rectangles of the puff pastry and refrigerate.

○ If using strawberries, destem and slice in half. Peel and core the apples, then slice them and the apricots.

apples
2 cups

apricots
2 cups

○ Arrange the fruit on the puff pastry as desired. Sprinkle with the sugar and bake for about 15 minutes, or until the edges are browned.

○ Serve warm or cold.

Demerara sugar
4 tablespoons

CHERRY TURNOVERS

 20 minutes prep time

 20 minutes baking time

 Serves 4

cherries
1 pound, frozen

Demerara sugar
¼ cup

cinnamon
1 pinch

egg
x 1

pie dough
2 sheets, packaged

○ Preheat the oven to 350°F and line a baking sheet with parchment paper.

○ In a large saucepan, stew the cherries with the sugar and cinnamon for 5 minutes. Let cool to room temperature. Meanwhile, beat the egg in a small bowl.

○ Cut out 8 rectangles of the pie dough and place them on the baking sheet. Place a heaping spoonful of cherries in the center of each, then fold over the dough to create mini "turnovers." Pinch edges to seal.

○ Brush with the beaten egg and bake for about 15 minutes, or until golden brown.

creamy treats

FONTAINEBLEAU

 10 minutes prep time

 No bake

 Serves 4

farmer cheese
10 ounces

powdered sugar
¼ cup

heavy cream
1¼ cups

mixed berries
2 cups

○ Line a metal strainer with a cheesecloth and place over a large bowl.

○ In a medium bowl, combine the farmer cheese and powdered sugar. In a separate medium bowl, firmly whip the cream while very cold, then fold into the cheese using a rubber spatula.

○ Pour the mixture into the cheesecloth, tightly close it up, and let strain for about 6 hours in the refrigerator.

○ Serve with the berries.

LEMON CURD

 10 minutes prep time

 5–8 minutes cooking time

 Makes 1⅓ cups

butter
½ cup

lemons
x 3

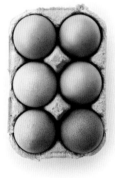

eggs
x 3

sugar
⅔ cup

○ Cut the butter into small cubes. Zest and juice the lemons. In a small saucepan, combine the eggs and sugar over low heat. Stir in the lemon juice and zest. Let thicken for 5–8 minutes.

○ Remove the saucepan from the heat and slowly stir in the butter until melted.

○ Strain over a large glass jar, then seal while warm. Refrigerate for at least 2 hours.

LEMON CREAM

 10 minutes prep time

 7–9 minutes cooking time

 Serves 4

lemons
x 3

double or heavy cream
2½ cups

sugar
1 cup

○ Zest and juice the lemons.

○ In a medium saucepan, heat the cream and sugar over low heat, stirring occasionally for 6–8 minutes. Then bring to a boil and cook for 1 minute.

○ Remove from the heat and stir in the lemon juice and zest. Pour into 4 small bowls or ramekins, and let set for at least 3 hours in the refrigerator.

HONEY MOUSSE

 20 minutes prep time

 No bake

 Serves 4

eggs
x 3

honey
⅓ cup, plus more for serving

ricotta
1⅔ cups

○ Separate the egg yolks and whites. In a double boiler, whip the yolks with the honey. Once fully combined, remove from the heat and stir in the ricotta.

○ In a medium bowl, beat the egg whites with a pinch of salt until lightly stiff, then gently fold into the ricotta mixture.

○ Let set for at least 3 hours in the refrigerator. Drizzle with honey to serve.

BLACKBERRY PEACH PARFAIT

 10 minutes prep time

 No bake

 Serves 4

peaches
x 2

Greek yogurt
24 ounces

blackberry jam
4 tablespoons

blackberry liqueur
(crème de mûre)
4 tablespoons

O Slice and peel the peaches.

O Divide the yogurt among 4 bowls.

O To a small bowl, add the blackberry jam and stir to soften it. Top the yogurt with the peach chunks and jam. Drizzle with the liqueur to serve.

TIRAMISU

 20 minutes prep time

 No bake

 Serves 4

eggs
x 3

sugar
½ cup

mascarpone
9 ounces

ladyfingers
x 16

strong coffee
½ cup

cocoa powder
4 tablespoons

○ Separate the egg yolks and whites. In a large bowl, beat the egg yolks and sugar with an electric mixer for 10 minutes, until it has roughly tripled in volume. Add the mascarpone and gently whip until the ingredients are evenly blended.

○ In a separate large bowl, beat the egg whites with a pinch of salt until lightly stiff, then fold into the mascarpone mixture.

○ Dip the ladyfingers in the coffee until lightly soaked and layer them in a 10 x 7-inch baking dish. Cover with a layer of the mascarpone mixture, then layer the remaining coffee-soaked ladyfingers next and finish with the remaining mascarpone on top. Sprinkle with the cocoa powder. Let set for 6 hours in the refrigerator.

CHEESECAKE CUPS

 20 minutes prep time

 No bake

 Serves 4

shortbread cookies
x 4

cream cheese
6 ounces

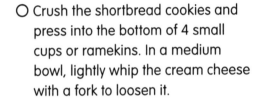

○ Crush the shortbread cookies and press into the bottom of 4 small cups or ramekins. In a medium bowl, lightly whip the cream cheese with a fork to loosen it.

○ In a separate medium bowl, firmly whip the cream while very cold, slowly adding in the powdered sugar. Gently fold into the cream cheese.

○ Juice and zest the lemon and add to the cream cheese mixture. Divide the mixture among the 4 cups. Refrigerate for at least 3 hours.

heavy cream
⅔ cup

powdered sugar
4 tablespoons

lemon
x ½

MUESLI YOGURT

 5 minutes prep time

 No bake

Serves 4

apricots or peaches
x 2

whole almonds
¼ cup

unsalted pistachios
¼ cup

Greek yogurt
24 ounces

○ Peel and cut the fruit into quarters and coarsely chop the almonds and pistachios.

○ Divide the yogurt among 4 small bowls. Drizzle with honey and top with the fresh fruit and nuts.

honey
4 teaspoons

creamy treats

RICE PUDDING

 10 minutes prep time

 45–60 minutes cooking time

 Serves 4

whole milk
2 pints

vanilla bean
x 1

Arborio rice
⅔ cup

sugar
½ cup

○ In a large saucepan, bring the milk and whole vanilla bean to a boil over medium-high heat. Then add the rice and reduce the heat to low. Cook for 45 minutes to 1 hour, stirring frequently. Remove from the heat.

○ Remove and discard the vanilla bean and stir in the sugar. Divide the pudding among 4 small bowls. Drizzle with honey and sprinkle with sliced almonds, if desired.

creamy treats

MAPLE RICOTTA

 10 minutes prep time

 No bake

 Serves 4

ricotta
2 cups

vanilla extract
1 teaspoon

O In a small bowl, combine the ricotta and vanilla.

O Divide the mixture among 4 small bowls and drizzle with maple syrup to serve.

maple syrup
to taste

RASPBERRY FROMAGE BLANC

🔪 **5 minutes prep time**

🍲 **No bake**

☺ **Serves 4**

fromage blanc
16 ounces

raspberries
2½ cups

dark chocolate chips
¼ cup

O Divide the fromage blanc among 4 small bowls.

O Add the raspberries and chocolate chips, and top with sugar or honey, if desired.

RASPBERRY CREAM SANDWICHES

 15 minutes prep time

 No bake

 Makes 8 sandwiches

heavy cream
¾ cup

mascarpone
1 tablespoon

○ In a medium bowl, firmly whip the cream and mascarpone together while very cold, slowly adding in the powdered sugar and vanilla.

○ Spread a generous amount of the cream mixture on 8 waffle cookies, then top each with raspberries and another cookie. Serve immediately.

powdered sugar
2 tablespoons

vanilla, powdered
1 pinch

waffle cookies
x 16

raspberries
2½ cups

LEMON MERINGUE ICE CREAM

✐ **10 minutes prep time**

🍲 **No bake**

☺ **Serves 4**

vanilla ice cream
4 cups

small meringues
x 6, packaged

○ Take the ice cream out of the freezer and let soften for 5 minutes. Coarsely chop the meringues.

○ In a 9 x 13-inch baking dish, quickly combine the ice cream, lemon curd, and meringues. Place the baking dish in the freezer and let set for at least 2 hours.

lemon curd (see page 101)
½-ounce jar

AFFOGATO

 10 minutes prep time

 No bake

 Serves 4

chocolate
3 ounces

hazelnuts
⅓ cup

vanilla ice cream
or frozen yogurt
4 cups

espresso
4 ounces

○ Chop or shave the chocolate with a knife and chop the hazelnuts.

○ Divide the ice cream among 4 mugs or heat-resistant glasses. Pour 1 ounce of espresso over each, then top with the chocolate and hazelnuts.

FROZEN RASPBERRY SMOOTHIE

 10 minutes prep time

No bake

☺ **Serves 4**

raspberries, frozen
1 pound

small bananas, sliced
x 2

○ Let the raspberries thaw for 10 minutes before using.

○ Blend the raspberries, bananas, and honey in a blender for 5 minutes, or until smooth and creamy. Serve immediately.

honey
1–2 tablespoons

MANGO FROZEN YOGURT

10 minutes prep time

No bake

Serves 4

frozen mango slices
x 4

stirred yogurt
12 ounces

honey
1 tablespoon

○ Chop the mango.

○ Blend the mango, yogurt, and honey in a blender until smooth. Let sit at room temperature for 1 minute if necessary, then blend again to get a creamy texture. Divide among 4 bowls. Serve immediately.

ROASTED-MARSHMALLOW SUNDAE

✎ **15 minutes prep time**

🍲 **1–2 minutes baking time**

☺ **Serves 4**

vanilla ice cream
4 cups

cookies of your choice
x 4

○ Let the ice cream soften for several minutes, and coarsely chop the cookies.

○ In a 9 x 13-inch baking dish, combine the ice cream and cookies until evenly distributed.

○ Arrange the marshmallows on top of the ice cream and broil for 1–2 minutes, until the tops of the marshmallows are lightly browned. Drizzle with chocolate sauce, if desired, and serve immediately.

marshmallows
1 package

CARAMEL CORN SUNDAE

 10 minutes prep time

 No bake

 Serves 4

dark chocolate
4 ounces

heavy cream
½ cup

peanuts
¼ cup

caramel squares
¼ cup

vanilla ice cream
4 cups

caramel popcorn
1 package

○ Chop the chocolate and place in a small bowl. In a small saucepan, bring the cream to a boil over medium-high heat, then pour over the chocolate. Stir until smooth. In a small nonstick skillet, toast the peanuts. Remove from the heat and allow to cool. Roughly chop the peanuts and caramel squares.

○ Divide the ice cream among 4 bowls. Sprinkle with the popcorn, chopped caramel, and peanuts. Drizzle with the chocolate sauce, if desired.

SPIKED COFFEE GRANITA

 15 minutes prep time

 No bake

 Serves 4

strong coffee, hot
2½ cups

sugar
⅓ cup

rum or liquor of choice
3 tablespoons

heavy cream
¾ cup

powdered sugar
1 tablespoon

○ In a medium bowl, mix the coffee and sugar until the sugar is dissolved, then spike with the liquor of your choice.

○ Pour into a heat-resistant storage container and freeze for at least 3 hours. Scrape with a fork every half hour to loosen.

○ Whip the cream while very cold, slowly adding in the powdered sugar. Divide the granita among 4 small bowls and top with the whipped cream.

ADULT STRAWBERRY SUNDAE

🔪 **15 minutes prep time**

🍲 **No bake**

☺ **Serves 4**

strawberries
1 pound

orange
x 1

Grand Marnier
1 tablespoon

Demerara sugar
3 tablespoons

vanilla ice cream
4 cups

○ Destem the strawberries, then cut into quarters. Zest and juice the orange.

○ In a medium bowl, combine the strawberries, orange juice and zest, Grand Marnier, and sugar, and cover with plastic wrap. Let marinate for 1 hour in the refrigerator.

○ Divide the strawberry mixture among 4 sundae cups or bowls and a scoop of ice cream. Top with whipped cream, if desired.

ICE CREAM SANDWICHES

 10 minutes prep time

 No bake

 Makes 8 sandwiches

ice cream flavor of choice
4 cups

shortbread cookies,
preferably thin
x 16

○ Line a baking sheet with parchment paper and place in the freezer.

○ Let the ice cream soften for 10 minutes, then loosen gently with a spatula, being careful not to let it melt.

○ Spread a generous amount of ice cream on 8 cookies, then top each with another cookie. Place on the baking sheet in the freezer. Let set for about 2 hours before serving.

FROZEN TIRAMISU

 20 minutes prep time

 No bake

 Serves 4

vanilla ice cream
1 quart

lemon
x ½

dark chocolate
2 ounces

strong coffee
½ cup

ladyfingers
x 12–16

○ Take the ice cream out of the freezer and let soften for 10 minutes. Zest the lemon and grate the chocolate.

○ In a medium bowl, combine the coffee and lemon zest, then dip the ladyfingers in the coffee.

○ In an 8 x 4-inch loaf pan, layer the soaked ladyfingers and ice cream. Continue layering until you run out of ingredients, ending with the ice cream. Top with the chocolate last and chill in the freezer for at least 4 hours.

Ingredient Index

Translation copyright © 2019 by Hachette Livre (Marabout)
Photographs copyright © 2019 by Valéry Guedes

Image credits © Shutterstock: Choco Cornflake Treats by GrigoryL; Blackberry Peach Parfait by Sofia Iartseva; Caramel Corn
Sundae by Olga Danylenko.

Library of Congress Cataloging-in-Publication Data
Names: Arnoult, Natacha, author. | Guedes, Valéry, photographer.
Title: Super easy sweets : 69 really simple dessert recipes / Natacha Arnoult ; photographs by Valéry Guedes.
Description: New York : Clarkson Potter/Publishers, 2019.
Identifiers: LCCN 2018045931 (print) | LCCN 2018047152 (ebook) | ISBN 9780525573265 | ISBN 9780525573258 (pbk.)
Subjects: LCSH: Desserts. | Baking. | LCGFT: Cookbooks.
Classification: LCC TX773 (ebook) | LCC TX773 .A77 2019 (print) | DDC 641.86--dc23
LC record available at https://lccn.loc.gov/2018045931

ISBN 978-0-525-57325-8
Ebook ISBN 978-0-525-57326-5

Printed in China

Cover photography by Valéry Guedes
Translation by Nicholas LoVecchio

10 9 8 7 6 5 4 3 2 1

First American Edition